THE Dad Difference

Claire Thurston

www.daddifference.com

ISBN 978-0-615-98005-8

Introduction

Congratulations, you're going to have a kid! Maybe you're totally pumped to raise that little boy or girl. Or maybe you've got no idea what to do and you've found yourself breaking out into sweats for NO REASON. There is no way to know what kind of Dad you'll be until it's happening, but one thing is for certain: Dads have the power to make a difference in their child's life.

This little book is a celebration of what it means to be a Dad. It consists of five simple things you can do with your child and why they are important.

The fact of the matter is that when it comes to raising children, our culture still doesn't have a good idea of the role that men can play. In the 1950's, mothers were stereotyped as smiling housewives which was a ridiculous over-simplification. Despite the progress made by the women's movement, one consequence has been the emergence of a new stereotype of dads as overgrown children or buffoons. That doesn't do us any good either.

Recent research has made it clear that Dads can have a profound and unique impact on the growth of their children. Families come in all shapes and combinations and whether you are raising a child on your own, with a spouse or with a partner, it's important to know that there are things Dads are just plain good at and that these things affect children in a positive way.

So Dad Up! Your adventure is just beginning and now there is a roadmap. This book is a start. Try these five things with your kid and let's see how it can change our world.

One: Be There.

Instructions: Just be there as much as you can. No minimum time required.

Here I am in my high chair....It's him!...Let me out!...Something exciting is about to happen!

The Dad Difference

Even at only eight weeks old, your baby already shows different responses to you and your spouse. Research results are in. With Mom, your baby relaxes and gets cozy. Kids just respond differently to Dads. When they see you, they get more alert, ready to join in the fun.

Here's a visual to illustrate the difference:

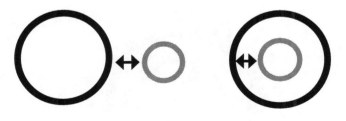

Father-Child   **vs.**   **Mother-Child**

You were never merged with your child during pregnancy. Your very separateness triggers a variety of positive impacts on your child:

Your child's sense of autonomy, personal power

Your child's self-reliance and self-control

Your child's empathy for others

Your child's values

For Your Child:

Your son or daughter will be more independent, curious and adventurous. And with a strong sense of "center" your child will be able to weigh choices and to resist peer pressure.

For You:

Your child will enjoy joining you in your adventures—whether it is a hike or trying new food. Your child will be more likely to play independently by your side if you have work to do. You will be able to trust your child's ability to think through and handle difficult situations.

For Your World:

As an adult, your child will be a more independent and creative thinker. That means innovative and sophisticated problem-solving as we confront challenges in the future.

Two: Pick up your baby your way.

Instructions: Pick up your baby. Move your baby one way. Hold to body. Move your baby another way. Hold to body.

I'm heading up...faster...slower...now I can see the ceiling...now I'm sideways! Coming closer to Dad, then out again...this is fun!

The Dad Difference

You like holding your baby in different ways and you like to create elaborate or challenging environments for your child to explore. You like changing things up. When your child is strong enough, you like to roughhouse and wrestle. You are stimulating your child's ability to adapt physically and emotionally to life.

For Your Child:

Your child is excited about life because you show the variety of experience. You stimulate intellectual curiosity too.

For You:

Both you and your child are getting better at communicating with each other and reading each other's cues. You have started a non-verbal dialogue with your child, which is the foundation for future talks. You know, "BIG talks."

For Your World:

As an adult, your son or daughter will be adaptable and will be able to work better in a team to solve problems.

Three: Toss your child in the air.

Instructions: Toss your child in the air. See giant smile. Hear squeals of delight. If you hear, "Again!" Repeat.

I'm in the air! I'm in the air! What's going to happen? Now I'm coming down into those strong arms. Oh, I'm safe again. I want to do that more!

The Dad Difference

You toss your son or daughter in the air then catch the child in safe arms. After the falling sensation, the embrace communicates that the world is a safe place and it is thrilling to be alive.

I'm unsure, I'm excited, I'm safe. I'm unsure, I'm excited, I'm safe.

You make your child feel comfortable in the world, especially in the exciting and as yet unknown world of other people.

For Your Child:

Your child will reach out to friends and enjoy them. Understanding the intriguing and expansive world of people will help develop compassion for others.

For You:

Your child will understand you, deepening the dialogue. Your child will also bring a circle of friends into your life, including classmates and their parents.

For Your World:

As an adult, your son or daughter will be empathetic towards others. This aspect of your influence is truly world transforming. More empathic people in society will create better and more peaceful relationships between individuals, families, neighbors, communities and nations.

Four: Wait for it.

Instructions: Watch your child work to master a new feat. Hear or see signs of frustration. Wait. Help if necessary.

Ugh, my body is so heavy... All I want to do is push myself up. Why is this so HARD? Why can't I get to that toy?! Oh look it's Dad. I'm gonna try a little harder.

The Dad Difference

When your child is attempting to crawl or walk or accomplish any skill, you wait to let your child work it out. Waiting to intervene helps your child to delay gratification.

For Your Child:

By learning how to delay gratification, your child will be able to accomplish goals without giving up too easily. Studying and doing homework or getting good at a sport requires discipline and discipline begins with being able to set aside what you want to do in the moment.

For You:

You can share in the pride of your child's accomplishments. In everyday situations that require waiting, like standing in line, your child will be more patient.

For Your World:

As an adult, your son or daughter will have the discipline to accomplish their goals. Society will improve as more citizens accomplish their positive individual achievements.

Five: Field the BIG Questions.

Instructions: If you know the answers, reply. If you don't know the answers, don't panic.

Wow, Dad knows everything. I want to know what he knows.

The Dad Difference

On the ceiling of the Sistine Chapel, Adam's hand stretches across the expanse towards God's hand. Your separate presence challenges your child to reach for ideals. Here is the good news: when your child asks you the BIG questions, you don't have to have all the answers, you just have to be a positive attentive presence. The most important thing that you can do is to allow your child to ask those questions. When your child looks at you with adoring eyes as if you were God, don't panic! The fact that your child feels comfortable coming to you with his or her questions is a good and natural thing.

For Your Child:

Ideals help your child believe in a world of possibility and significance. A sense of the world's significance inspires your child to contribute. Applying values in difficult situations helps your child to develop character.

For You:

Living your values brings your child closer to you and enhances receptivity to those values. If you are involved in a religious tradition, you play a strong role in passing along that tradition.

For Your World:

As an adult, your son or daughter's strong personal character and clear sense of values will improve our world.

What Difference Does a Dad Make?

- You strengthen your child's sense of self and self-control, which leads to more considered choices.

- You foster your child's independence.

- You make your child feel safe to explore, to risk trying new things.

- You enhance your child's ability to understand and empathize with others, which attracts and builds friendships now and as an adult. Your child will be less likely to objectify others.

- You help your child to resist peer pressure.

- You mobilize your child's moral development and aspiration.

- You inspire your child to live up to the family's highest values.

What Difference Does a Dad Make?

This is good news for parents: good news for fathers to understand their importance to their family, their community and their world and good news for mothers who stand to benefit through more father involvement.

This new data on father's role has not yet become mainstream. But when it does, the implications will affect every aspect of society, from the father-child relationship itself, to marriage, family, the workplace, social ills, culture and the law. Untold discoveries become possible while a wide range of social problems will gain improved treatment and prevention. That's the Difference a Dad makes. ◆

About the Author

On trying to understand fatherhood in America, I have come to believe that fathers remain an untapped transformational force. With findings from new research demonstrating father's impact, family relationships will strengthen while a wide range of social problems will find improved treatment and prevention strategies.

—Claire Thurston

Claire Thurston has been researching father's role in child development for 25 years and she presents workshops at hospitals, schools and conferences. She is a regular "Dads and Families" columnist for the online magazine The Good Men Project, which receives over six million views per month. Recent articles include: *"What is the Dad Difference?"* and *Historical Parenting: The Fathers of Nelson Mandela.*

The Denver area probation departments piloted her protocol, the Paternal Empathy Program to prevent child abuse. In 2004 she was awarded the Presidential Management Fellowship and helped to develop The LEAD (Leadership Education and Development) Certificate Program for the Federal Government. She was a board member then staff member of Family Network, a non-profit for rebuilding intergenerational family support systems in San Francisco, California. She received her Bachelors from Brown University and Masters from the University of Colorado.

Article links:
http://goodmenproject.com/families/what-is-the-dad-difference/

http://goodmenproject.com/families/nelson-mandela-wwh/

Made in the USA
Middletown, DE
26 January 2018